The Shift

What it is...

Why it's happening...

How it is affecting you and

the mastering of Alchemy

Jim Self

Dedicated to all who are asking and allowing.

CHAPTER 1

The Shift. What is it?

We've been hearing about "The Shift" for so long, it's hard to believe that it's finally here! But what precisely is shifting? What are we moving from? What are we moving toward? And – more importantly – what difference is it really going to make to your world... your life... your family... your loved ones... and you?

Have you noticed that...

Time seems to be speeding up?

Your memories aren't as reliable as they used to be?

Stuff you thought you had dealt with is suddenly resurfacing?

And nothing seems to be working the way it used to?

You are not alone!

If you have been hearing people talk about moving from the Third Dimension to the Fifth Dimension but you haven't a clue how that's going to come about, or what specific changes it's going to bring, or even what the Fifth Dimension is – you are not alone. Moreover, it's no accident that you're reading this book at this moment. It was written for you.

The purpose of this book is twofold: first, to present you with a container for much of the information that you already know, but may not be consciously aware that you know. And second, to introduce you to a set of tools, skills and opportunities that will enable you to build a platform that will allow you to step from a third-dimensional unconsciousness into a higher dimensional awareness, fully conscious, and completely realigned with who you are and who you have always been, but don't remember at this moment.

It is actually quite simple to create happiness, abundance and well-being in your life. As with so many aspects of life, however, that which is simple is sometimes the hardest to grasp. For example, the four-step formula for creation is truly this simple:

1. Create an Intention
2. Place your Attention on your Intention
3. Add an emotion such as happy, amused or excited to what you have your attention on and
4. The Universe, through the Law of Attraction, will give to you precisely what you placed your Attention upon. Your job is to receive it... to allow it to come to you to let yourself have what you just asked for.

In other words, "Ask and it shall be given unto you."

So - why are most of us unable to follow this simple formula and create the lives we desire?

The noise of the third-dimension is very distracting, pulling our attention into the past or projecting it into the future, where fear and anxiety often reside. When emotions such as worry, doubt, and lack arise, holding our attention on our intention to be happy can become very challenging. The Law of Attraction gives us exactly what we place our attention on; it doesn't understand: "Just give me the good stuff." So how you hold your emotions and thoughts is how the Universe understands your asking. "Ask and you shall receive."

There is a Shift, a transformation, a really BIG change occurring.

This Shift that is underway is affecting every aspect of our third-dimensional reality. This Shift is so far-reaching that our limited imagination cannot begin to grasp the transition and the changes we are now in the midst of experiencing. This Shift is affecting every aspect of life on this planet – our political, social and economic structures, the environment, institutions and wars, how we view our relationships and our work. Simply put, every thought we think and every feeling we feel. It is altering time, our memory, our DNA, the wiring of our physical and emotional bodies, our beliefs, our perceptions of good and bad, right and wrong. Most especially, this Wave of Change is affecting our awareness of what is possible. It is offering us abundant, new understandings, instructions and possibilities of how to once again live in harmony with each other, the environment and All That Is.

However, between where we currently exist and this new higher dimension of "Heaven on Earth," where we will soon arrive, there is a bit of a gap ...

Becoming aware of becoming aware

The "Shift in consciousness" that is occurring is a shift in our very perception of our world. As most of us have played this game of life, we have tried to fit in and to follow the rules. We have tried to create a better life for ourselves and for our families. However, in our rush to create more for ourselves - the bigger house, better car, higher salary, etc., many of us have discovered that we have actually created less. We have less time to spend in that big house, less time to enjoy the company of our family and friends and less opportunity to appreciate a sunset or take pleasure in the natural beauty that surrounds us. Many people have begun to feel that something is not right, that something valuable has been lost. What is really missing, whether we are aware of it or not, is that we all have lost a part of our "selves" along the way. And at the end of the day, more, bigger and better has still not been enough. We have disconnected from the things that truly nourish us and it has left us physically ill, emotionally unhappy, mentally exhausted and spiritually unclear about who we truly are.

This is now beginning to change.

As more and more of us are awakening, we are beginning to remember who we are. We are recognizing imbalances in our lives and we are asking ourselves: "What's really important to me? What truly makes me happy?" The answer isn't found through gaining more of the world outside, but in gaining more of the "me" within.

In our rush to the top we left a part of ourselves behind. We traded respect for competition, kindness for advantage, and giving for taking. We lost touch with our "Inner Guidance," which has always directed us to a higher, more aligned place. This higher place is a place where cooperation, support and understanding create deeper trust, friendship and compassion.

The Shift is occurring within the Hearts of ALL of humanity and millions are beginning to awaken. It is an "awakening of consciousness!" It is taking place across the world in every town and village and in the Hearts of each child, woman and man. We are finding a new passion within, and we are beginning to recognize that who we are counts. We ALL matter, and we ALL have a contribution to make. This awakening consciousness has no limits. It is a shift that is taking us all into a higher dimensional awareness; a higher, more aligned way of life. We are "becoming aware of becoming aware."

The new Waves of Light

Two massive Waves of Light and Energy are moving through the Universe, through the Earth and through each of us. These Waves of change are working together in perfect synchronization, evolving everything to a higher consciousness.

One Wave is expanding outward, as an ever-widening ripple on a pond, spreading greater Light, knowledge and wisdom, opening ever-expanding gateways to higher consciousness and evolution. This Wave is shifting mass consciousness from the third-dimensional perspective, through the fourth, into a fifth-dimensional perspective. This Wave is creating a fifth-dimensional community of higher consciousness on Earth that is realigning us with the All That Is.

As this first Wave accelerates it is fascinating to observe how it is powerfully and positively affecting us. This Wave is providing us with choices and presenting us with possibilities that have not been available to us before. This Wave is also making it possible for the second Wave to unlock all that has been keeping us stuck in the third-dimension.

The second Wave operates very differently than the first. Its function is to create harmony. However, in order to achieve harmony, everything that is not of the Light, everything that does not exist in well-being and balance, is being destabilized, dissolved and cleared away. Everything that is not aligned in our lives is being loosened and released.

This Wave is releasing all dysfunctional patterns on every level. All that is lacking in integrity will dissolve to be replaced with new patterns of energy, Light, knowledge and wisdom that are available in the first Wave. In short, as one Wave of Light is emptying the vessel, the other Wave of Light is refilling it.

These transformative Waves are allowing all of us to re-wire, re-connect, re-align and re- member who we are and what we really came here to accomplish. Like a tsunami, these Waves are significantly stepping up in intensity. We will see tremendous transitions in the upcoming months and years.

Why is this all happening now?

This is all happening now because we have asked for it to occur. It is also happening now because we have succeeded, in the most amazing way, in accomplishing what we came here to achieve by playing this Game of the third-dimension. And it is now time to remember, to return Home to the Heart of the Creator, the All That Is. So, should you be happy? Yes! Should you be excited? Yes! Is it simple? Yes! Is it going to be easy? Not exactly... but it does not have to be difficult either.

We are playing in very exciting times, and in order to make this transition as easy as possible, we will need some new skills and tools to help us ride these Waves with grace and ease. We also will need a new understanding as to how to perceive our surroundings differently, and how to choose the reality we wish to experience.

CHAPTER 2

How it Might Be Affecting You

Time is going faster

Many people are not aware of the precise nature of the changes they are experiencing, but they are noticing the effects of these changes. For example, if you ask the question: "Do you think time is going faster?" Many will say "Yes, it is as if I just got out of bed in the morning, and before I know it I'm getting ready for bed again. Where did the day go?"

Time is more related to the rhythms and cycles held within our four lower bodies than it is to the clock on the wall. As these two massive Waves of Light flow within, through, and around us and the Earth, the reference points that we have come to know ourselves by are all changing.

The first change that is occurring is in the Earth's magnetic fields. The Waves of Light are altering the magnetic fields that surround the Earth, causing them to weaken, deteriorate and change. As the Earth's magnetic fields change, the magnetic fields, cycles and rhythms within our spiritual, mental, emotional and physical bodies are also being altered. Some cycles are accelerating while other cycles and rhythms are slowing down. Our concept of time is being altered as the

Waves of Light pass through each of us, changing the rhythms and cycles within.

Although the internal sensation is that time is going faster, we are actually losing time; time is not going faster, rather, it is collapsing into a single moment of Present Time, NOW.

For example, if it took you five minutes to walk from point A to point B, and you did this every day of your life, you would have a physical body sense of how long it takes you to cover the distance. But as time collapses, you have less time to walk the same length from A to B, so you now have a physical sense of having to walk faster to cover the same distance, even though your watch still shows the same amount of time was taken. What's happening is that your internal sensory mechanisms are telling you that time is going faster because you had to hurry to get to the same place in the same time that your watch actually recorded.

As the Waves of Light are changing our internal rhythms they are bringing us closer and closer to Present Time. Present Time is the only place in which we exist. And as our internal magnetic fields weaken, our cycles and rhythms are beginning to align in a singular flow of consciousness. Our biorhythms, heartbeats, and pulses of the meridian system are all beginning to align into a singular rhythm, aligning with the heart-beat of the Earth. As this occurs, all of our memories, thoughts, emotions and beliefs that are not aligned with the higher consciousness of well-being are falling away.

One Wave is clearing away many of our memories of the past; all those old arguments, embarrassing moments, and painful experiences stored unconsciously within our memory that have nothing to do with who we are and thus have no value in the present moment. Simultaneously, the other Wave of Light is expanding the range of possibilities within each of our realities, thereby providing more choice and opportunities to experience ourselves to the very fullest.

Losing your memories, gaining your truth

Have you noticed yourself beginning to say something, only to realize that you suddenly can't find the words to complete your sentences? Or that you can't recall the word for the spoon that you are holding in your hand? If this is happening to you, don't be alarmed. You're not the only one having these experiences. And no, it is not Alzheimer's. Neither does it have anything to do with your gender, age or culture.

The purpose of this second Wave of Light is to clear away old patterns, beliefs, thoughts and emotions that we hold that do not support our well-being. Because we did not know what to do with insults or invalidations that we received growing up, we learned to store away the uncomfortable and unsupportive thoughts and emotions that we experienced. In so doing, we chose to give up our own seniority, along with the truths and beliefs that we naturally held in well-being, and instead chose to believe other people's opinions.

As we begin to awaken and remember who we are, many of our old non-truth, non-aligned belief patterns are beginning to fall away. In this process we are losing many of our memories and our reference points upon which we have built our third-dimensional reality. These are falling away because we cannot take our negative thoughts, beliefs and emotions with us on this journey. The second Wave of Light is clearing them from our unconsciousness. As these unconscious reference points that support our sense of lack are being cleared, simple words like "spoon" sometimes get caught in the clearing of the patterns.

There is nothing broken. It is simply that who we are NOT and never were is beginning to fall away.

Simultaneously, the first Wave of Light is passing through us, expanding our awareness and our understanding of who we are, who we have always been. This understanding is not located in the analytical, rational mind. It is centered in our broader field of perception within our knowingness, within our higher consciousness and the Internal Guidance System found within our Hearts. As we are beginning to remember who we are, we are beginning to let go of who-we-are-not. And although letting go of who-we-are-not is very desirable, letting go of our beliefs, our thoughts and concepts of the world may not be an easy experience.

The transformation that is occurring within us is shifting our thoughts and beliefs, and changing the ways in which we experience the world around us. Until now, most of us have measured ourselves by the outside world. Our beliefs about how we look, what is acceptable, what we think, and how we act have all been influenced and established by the third-dimensional world outside ourselves.

Our thoughts create our beliefs, our beliefs create our habits and our habits create our lives. Our beliefs then connect the thoughts that run through our experiences, forming our conclusions. However, many of the thoughts that we think and the beliefs that we hold are actually not our own thoughts or beliefs; they were given to us by mom, dad, teacher, minister and the third-dimensional reality out-side of ourselves. It's not that mom and dad or anyone else around us set out deliberately to mislead us; they were simply passing on what their parents and their parent's parents (along with most of the rest of society) had taught them to accept as the "truth." Growing up, many of us may have intuitively felt that what others accepted as the "truth" did not feel "right" to us, but consensus opinion is a powerful thing. It's not easy to stand against the crowd or argue with our elders, or loved ones. Hence, many of us learned to "toe the line," to repress our intuitive senses, and dumb down our feelings. In the process, we became numb. This is why so many people today are unhappy, but have no idea why. It's because we have lost touch with our own inner guidance system.

Now, as we begin to awaken, a new recognition is unfolding within us. As we start to seek our own truth and walk our own unique path, many of us are beginning to realize that there is much more to who we are than the outside world has led us to believe. As we look within, we are beginning to realize that we are multi-dimensional, spiritual beings able to align with a Higher Truth. As this transformation is occurring, we are beginning to recognize that it is our own truth that creates happiness, success and balanced health, while adding simplicity to our life path.

In the past, only a few souls have experienced this Higher Truth. But now this truth has turned into an adventure that is being sought by many. Because of you, and the many others who are now awakening, a new consciousness is unfolding! The third-dimensional world that was defined by the truths, structures and beliefs of those around us is no longer working and is being dissolved. We are experiencing a huge change, a quickening in conscious awareness.

A Grand Awakening!

CHAPTER 3

What Are the Third and Fourth-Dimensions?

Many of us know, or intuitively feel, that there is a restructuring or movement going on, but few of us have sufficient information to make sense of these feelings. Quite simply, we are stepping out of a third-dimensional reality, passing through the fourth and are on our way to the fifth-dimension. But what are the dimensions?

Dimensions are not places. Rather, they are levels of consciousness, each with its own characteristics and ways of thinking, feeling and experiencing. Understanding the aspects, rules and structures of the third and fourth-dimensions gives us the opportunity to step from the noise of the third-dimension and its rigid structures into a more fluid set of choices held within the fourth.

In order to make this simple, let's consider the third and the fourth-dimensions each as a box. These two boxes overlap one another, allowing us to move from one box to the other. We have actually been living in the third and fourth-dimensions simultaneously for well over 60 years. One box holds noise, rigidity, and uncomfortable emotions, while the other box holds choice, beauty, well-being and appreciation. You have experienced yourself in both these boxes. But without a clear definition of what occurs in each box, it becomes difficult to understand and master yourself even in the best of situations. By knowing the difference between the two boxes a person can choose to live the life they wish to live, rather than simply reacting to life as it arrives on their doorstep each morning. By describing the characteristics of each box, we can develop a better understanding of how to choose.

CHAPTER 4

The Third-Dimensional Box and Structures

Form

First, the Earth, the mountains, the rivers, the lamp, the chair and the flowers that surround us are not the third-dimension. These are aspects of Form. Form is the result of density. Form has shape, mass, texture and weight that exists in both the third and the fourth-dimensions.

Here's the first useful piece that is not obvious. Form is also held within our thoughts and the emotions. Although it is not seen as physical density, heavy, ugly thoughts will produce a response. Additionally, light, airy, beautiful thoughts will produce a very different feeling or response.

For example, have you ever accepted someone else's opinion that you've done something "wrong" or are to blame for something, and then found yourself walking around with a heavy uncomfortable feeling of guilt? This guilt or blame is called a thought-form. How you choose to observe and hold that thought-form will influence your state of mind, emotions and even your physical health. It also determines your ability to successfully create your life, or not.

Heavier, emotionally charged thoughts are held in the third-dimensional reality, whereas light, airy, beautiful thought-forms are held in the fourth-dimension.

Three aspects of the third-dimension

Let's explore the characteristics that are found within the third-dimension. Remember, this is a box that holds a portion of your life experience.

In order to fully understand all that is about to be said, it is very helpful to understand the "Law of Attraction." Now, you might say, "But I already know all about the Law of Attraction." But believing you know about the Law of Attraction and living the Law of Attraction are two very different experiences.

The Law of Attraction says: "What you place your attention upon, I, the Universe, which adores you, will provide for you." The Law of Attraction is so important it is the foundation of EVERYTHING you have ever experienced.

The Law of Attraction does not understand words. It does not understand "please" and "thank you" in English, French, or any other language. The Law of Attraction understands the thought and the emotional vibrations you hold, both consciously and unconsciously. If you believe something is or you believe something is not, the Law of Attraction will respond accordingly. If you amplify your thoughts or beliefs with a charge of emotion, the Law of Attraction will provide you with more of the same in a quicker, fuller manner. What you put your attention on with a **charged emotion is what you will receive. Absolutely guaranteed.**

Time in the third-dimension

Most of humanity has been taught and believes that time is fixed and linear - past, present, future, and then you die. Although this is the generally accepted belief, it is incorrect. In the third-dimension time operates as a loop. It consists of a flow of thoughts and experiences that we label positive or negative. Either we embrace these experiences and hope they happen again or we resist them and hope they do not. To keep it simple, we take our past experiences and project them into our future and then step into that experience in a future-present-time moment to feel it all over again in a different size, shape or color.

Let me give you two examples. First, let us say that I was told that if I would become a lawyer, doctor, teacher or nurse I would be successful and happy. And although it may not feel correct inside, I agree. I then take that information and place it out in front of me, and follow that belief into the future. A belief is seldom experienced in the present moment, but projected out into a future.

Second, and this is perhaps a more important example, let us say that I once had a relationship that was the best of the best...until it was not. My lover left, telling me I was a terrible person, I would never succeed, I was not nice, and I did not have anything to offer to create a successful relationship with him or her. I was hurt. I felt rejected, and I went into a deep state of grief. Although I tried to get over the experience, I could not let it go, nor could I understand how I could be such a terrible a person. Eventually I made the decision that I was OK, at least on the surface, and I never wanted to meet someone like that again because I did not want to be hurt again. So I scream to the Universe, "God, never let this kind of experience happen to me again. If a person of that type ever comes anywhere near me, please warn me and put up big red flags so I don't get hurt again."

Can you see how I took a bad period from my past and placed it into my future, and then added a big dose of emotionally charged pain, fear and avoidance in order to protect myself?

The Law of Attraction does not understand the words NO, Don't and Stop. It understands only what we hold our attention upon. And because the Universe and the Law of Attraction adore me, and it is the Universe's passion to satisfy my every request, guess what I found on my door step the next morning ... and the next and the next and the next? With each step into the next Present Time moment I experience precisely what I asked for through my vibration. In other words, if the vibrations of my thoughts and emotions are negative, I get exactly what I put my attention upon. "I will provide you with exactly what you ask for," smiles the Law of Attraction.

So, third-dimensional time is not a structure; it is an application that allows us to create a new set of experiences based on our past to be experienced in our future. In the third-dimension there is a small sliver of the present time, known as Reactionary Present Time. In this sliver we step into the future that we resisted, finding ourselves in Present Time reacting to what we swore we never again wanted to experience. This is how time works in the third-dimensional box. In the third-dimension, choice is not a choice, because choice does not exist in the third-dimension.

Also built into the structure of third-dimensional time is a wonderful mechanism that can keep us out of great difficulty. A buffer, or lag in time, gives us the chance to reconsider the consequences of our actions, reactions, thoughts and emotions before we react and create something that we might have to clean up or apologize for afterwards. This built-in structure allows us a moment of pause in which to consider an action. During the Shift, however, this time buffer is dissolving. Many people are finding that things are now starting to manifest faster than they ever have before. In our future Present Time moments this buffer will cease to exist. What you ask for is what you will get... right now ... in exactly the form you think it.

Duality

Another important aspect of the third-dimension is Duality. Living within the field of duality was simply meant to provide us with a broad array of choices and opportunities in order to "know ourselves." Duality is a predominant structure of perception. Before the Fall of Consciousness, a long time ago, the purpose of duality was to assist us to learn how to walk in balance while experiencing contrast. If everything were blue there would be no contrast. Once red is brought in along with blue we now have contrast. Contrast was created to provide us with experiences for choice, such as hot and cold, large and small, bright and dull, etc.

As we began to experience third-dimensional consciousness, we added into duality the concepts of right and wrong, good and bad, and should and should not. When we lived in the higher fourth-dimension and above there was no good and bad or right and wrong. There was no judgment. Nothing was broken. There was nothing to fear. There were just simple choices of contrast giving us more ways to experience and know ourselves.

But with the Fall of Consciousness came fear, judgment and separation. We learned "us and them" and we learned to resist "them." These concepts of judgment, separation, good and bad, right and wrong and should/should not created a rigid, unforgiving structure that does not allow for flexibility or choice. This third-dimensional belief system bound our thoughts and emotions, creating extreme beliefs in "never" and "always"; rigid thought forms with very little opportunity for change, ease or well-being. In this rigid belief system of heavy thought-form, fear and pain were anchored. This is what the second Wave of Light is beginning to neutralize and remove from our memory as we prepare to step into the higher dimensions.

The Rational Mind

Our analytical, reasoning thought process is known as the rational mind. When we experienced the Fall of Consciousness we lost access to a great portion of our ability to perceive the reality around us. As we learned to experience fear of the past and worry of the future we lost the use of many of our spiritual abilities along with access to over 90% of the operational function within the brain, hence creating our rational mind.

The development of the rational mind has served us well in this environment. Its purpose has become to keep us safe and have us fit in. Due to fear and misuse, however, the rational mind operates more in limitation than it does in possibility and opportunity. Because we have given assignments to the mind that it was not designed for, our awareness and spiritual ranges of choice have greatly diminished. While the logical mind is a wonderful tool for measuring, comparing and making decisions, it only knows what it knows and has lost access to what it does not know. For thousands of years the rational mind has kept humanity tightly focused in the three-dimensional realm. This is now changing.

The three structures of this third-dimensional box are critical to our understanding. These three energetic structures – The Time Loop, Duality and the Rational

Mind - are intricately woven into the fabric of the third-dimensional matrix. By becoming aware of the underlying templates from which the third-dimension operates, we can begin to have the choice to step out of the third-dimension. We can re-construct and remember a significant part of ourselves, thereby freeing us to move beyond the limits of the third-dimension and opening the possibilities of the higher fourth and fifth-dimensions.

CHAPTER 5

The Fourth-Dimensional Box and Structures

As we begin to wake up and become conscious of being conscious, we also begin to experience options and choices that are not available to us in the third-dimension. The components of the fourth-dimensional box are actually very simple, but because we spend so much time in motion, reacting to our past and worrying about our future, we spend very little time in the present. Because of this pull between our past and future, it is difficult to become quiet enough to hold our attention on the simplicity of the life that is before us.

In the third-dimension, the Law of Attraction responds to the noise, motion and reaction we hold within us, giving back to us more of the same. By understanding and living three aspects of the fourth-dimension, we interrupt all those largely unconscious emotionally charged reactions and instead consciously choose the outcome we desire, thereby allowing the Law of Attraction to give us the new, positive desires.

Present Time

Learning to experience yourself in the present moment is the single most important choice you can make in moving forward on your journey.

Where third-dimensional present time is a charged reactionary moment influenced by our past, our fourth-dimensional Present Time is a quiet NOW moment. We only exist in the Now, but most of us hold very little of our attention here. We are consumed by past experiences and projected worries, yet, paradoxically, because we do not understand the structures of the dimensions, it is precisely this fear-based state of thought and emotion that keeps us bound to the third-dimension.

In the fourth-dimension, past and future time change significantly. The past simply becomes a neutral experience, or an historic event for reference. Yesterday's pain has no bearing on tomorrow. The information, knowledge and wisdom gained from the past assist us in making better decisions about our current and future well-being. The present is all there is. You can plan for future events using information gathered from the past, but the decisions become conscious choices made in this present moment. While the future is an opportunity waiting to be fashioned, it is in this NOW moment that choices are made.

Choice

In the fourth-dimension, reaction is replaced by choice, providing flexibility and new possibilities. With choice you have an opportunity to observe, and to experience and choose without judgment, right or wrong, good or bad, or the fear of being punished. Fourth-dimensional conscious choice gives you the opportunity to make mistakes and then correct the situation without blame or guilt.

Conscious choice invites a wider range of possibilities, allowing for well-being, happiness and realignment within the Heart. It is in the fourth-dimension that you get to take back your power to choose. You can make better decisions from a platform of focused clarity, certainty and an awareness of your own personal presence. As the third-dimensional good and bad, right and wrong fall away, an ever-expanding sense of capability begins to re-awaken within you. Choice creates opportunity. Opportunity allows for well-being. Well-being awakens happiness, openness and the inner smile within the Heart. From your open Heart, your purpose and the fulfillment of all your dreams are within your grasp.

Higher Concepts

As you become conscious of being conscious in this fourth-dimensional reality, many higher concepts of life become available, allowing you to move around with greater ease and understanding. One of these higher concepts is Paradox. Paradox, simply stated, is, What was true a moment ago may not be true in this NOW moment, and what was false a moment ago may no longer be false in this moment.

Because of the fears, pain and distrust that we all have stored in our unconsciousness, we hold many rigid beliefs about the world around us and those who live within it. We hold these beliefs anchored in words such as ALWAYS and NEVER. "He will always be bad. She will never change. I will never forgive them." As the past pains of the third-dimension are dragged into the future, our tendency is to react the same way this time as we reacted the last time, thereby repeating the experiences of the past once again.

As we consciously recognize that we have choices about the world around us, incorporating the concept of paradox allows the past to be past and frees the future for new opportunity. Paradox allows us to recognize a person or situation as it occurred in the past; however, it now provides the opportunity to observe the person or situation in this moment, allowing them to be who they are now, rather than us observing them through the limitations of the our past reactions.

As Paradox loosens up the rigidity of the past, the higher concept of Allowing opens up broader opportunities for you to experience. Allowing is a powerful concept; it does not imply weakness, or inability, but rather, simply enables you to recognize the situation before you, and provides you with a present time choice to create a better opportunity for a desirable outcome.

As you begin to recognize the many tools, skills, concepts and opportunities the fourth- dimension provides, your life will change. You can choose to step out of habits of reaction and restriction. Trust becomes a choice. The need to experience lack, weakness, fear and doubt falls rapidly away as the structures of the fourth-dimension are understood and practiced. What we considered to be mere words in the third-dimension now become concepts with a fuller, deeper meaning, and a more rounded flow and experience in the fourth. Words such as Happy, Certainty, Seniority, Presence, Capable, Gracious and Commanding are no longer intellectual thoughts, but rather, become important internal sensations and feelings guided by your Heart.

These concepts can only be felt and lived in the Present Time moment. As you remember and re-own these feelings and sensations, you re-ignite the Internal Guidance System within your Heart. And as other higher, vibrant concepts become internalized, felt and demonstrated within your life, a transformation occurs in how you present and experience yourself. These words are more than concepts. They are Living Words. They are energetic building blocks that we will discuss in a later chapter. As you begin to wear and experience these words they weave together, like a well-tailored suit of clothes, creating a new ease and a brighter presence. You no longer give away your power. You now begin to choose and create from these higher vibrations the life you wish to experience.

This is our natural state of being. However, becoming conscious, aware and holding a well-grounded sense of self requires a shift in our habits and beliefs. Since childhood, most of us have been invalidated in our third-dimensional experience. We have not been taught, nor encouraged, nor often even allowed to make decisions from our own naturally balanced places of certainty, trust and passion. Instead, most of us have been taught to fear, doubt and mistrust the world around us. Consequently, we have not fully experienced who we came here to be.

Alignment and Balance

The reality that we know as the third-dimension is a classroom of sorts where we are participating in the ever-expanding evolutionary cycle of our spiritual growth. In order to play in this classroom, we have had to forget ourselves, to leave much of our wisdom, knowledge and many of our great skills behind.

In short, the third-dimension is a classroom of IMBALANCE.

Our purpose, or mission, is to rediscover and master BALANCE

However, since by definition the third-dimension is IMBALANCE, balance can never be found in the third-dimension; it can only be found by stepping out of the third-dimension. And this doorway is the fourth-dimension.

Very few rules exist in the fourth-dimension; it is open, receptive, and allowing of all possibilities. It is a dimension of choice and observation and it operates as a flexible platform without the rigidity of the third dimensional box. The fourth-dimension provides us with an opportunity to reframe our reference points, review our beliefs and attain a new understanding of what is possible. It allows us "to be in the world but not of the third-dimensional world."

The fourth-dimension is the stepping-stone to the higher dimensions; it provides us with an opportunity for movement toward a "higher way of life" – a life of community, cooperation and co-creation.

As long ago as the 16th Century, William Shakespeare wrote "All the world's a stage, and all the men and women merely players." Shakespeare wasn't just a great playwright; he was a very wise man, for life on this planet is indeed a Grand Play. And now we are coming to the end of Act 3 – the Final Act. This is where we get to bring our Grand Play to its finale and go Home.

Going Home is precisely what the Shift is all about. The Shift is clearing away all that we are not, and assisting us in rewiring the connections, so that we can finally remember **all that we are.**

However, this is not going to happen all on its own, without any effort on our part. In order to complete this wonderful Game we are going to have to put our Selves back together again. This is where Mastering Alchemy comes in. This is where learning to re-create our personal power fields with the tools of sacred geometry finally comes into play.

CHAPTER 6

Tools to Rebuild Yourself

Re-claiming your Command Center

Understanding who we are requires that we bring ourselves into a Present Time focus. There is a place within the center of our heads that acts as a Command Center, a place where clear decisions can be made and actions can be set into motion. However, as we grew up and learned to trust the opinions and beliefs of others, we stepped away, as it were, from the center of our heads and gave away our seniority to those who said they had a better idea of life than we did. Reclaiming the center of our heads is necessary if we are to move forward.

Whose thoughts and emotions are these? The true gift of grounding

As we have learned, many of the thoughts we think and the emotions we feel passing through us each day do not even belong to us. Thoughts are electrical and the emotions are magnetic. In addition to helping realign us to our own personal frequency, rebuilding our grounding mechanism is invaluable in clearing away these thoughts and emotions. There are two components to grounding. One consists of an electrical line that runs from the first chakra to the center of the Earth, which grounds non-aligned electrical thought. The second consists of a coil of energy that wraps around the electrical grounding line and runs all the way down to the center of the Earth. Its purpose is to clear away all the emotions that do not belong to you.

Sacred Geometry - rebuilding your Personal Power Field with the Octahedron

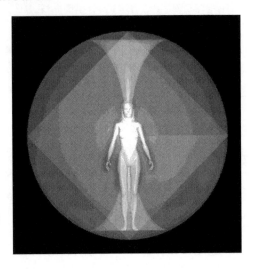

Once we have grounded ourselves, the next step is to rebuild the geometric containment field. The aura or personal energy field was originally held within a series of geometric shapes. The first and least complex geometric shape to be rebuilt is known as the Octahedron. This geometric shape has the appearance of diamond, or four-sided pyramid, pointing up, placed on top of a four-sided pyramid pointing down. The Octahedron acts as an antenna aligning and reconnecting us with our own higher dimensional frequency of consciousness.

By recreating this geometric shape, we begin to put into place the necessary structure to rebuild our Personal Power Field. This is done by creating a column of Light that moves from a point beneath us upward through the central core of our bodies, surrounding the chakras and extending to a point above our heads. (see diagram). As this flow of Light continues to extend upward through the column and out the top, it accelerates around the Octahedron and then flows back into the bottom of the column to accelerate upwards again. This accelerated flow of Light then creates a stabilized platform of consciousness that opens up opportunities to "Know One's Self" as a Higher Dimensional Being.

CHAPTER 7

Where It's Taking You

From this awareness, we once again become able to regain Balance within our masculine and feminine energy fields. This starts with an expanded consciousness communication with Gaia, the Earth consciousness and with the Grids of Light surrounding the Earth, known as the Ascension Grids. As the Earth's energy flows up through the central column within our body, a sphere of Light is formed, enabling a reconnection with the higher dimensional feminine nature of the Mother-God. This allows the reconnection to all aspects of the Divine Feminine that we lost in the Fall of Consciousness.

Through the connection with the Ascension Grid, the Masculine Nature of the Father-God is then brought down through the central column of our body, and then flows out and around us, creating a perfect Masculine sphere of symmetry that surrounds our body, allowing a balanced integration of Masculine energy to become available to us.

Entering the Higher Mind

From this level of consciousness, we can now accelerate the surrounding fields of Light to a velocity approaching the speed of Light. Not a difficult thing to do. From this higher, faster frequency, an opening into an alignment of Light known as the Higher Mind now becomes available to us. The Higher Mind is vast. Although entering the Higher Mind is not difficult, mastery of the Higher Mind is an eternal unfolding.

The Higher Mind is quiet. There is a detachment from the world around us. There is focus, clarity, a curiosity, but no questions are asked. It is through the Higher Mind that conscious contact with the Soul begins, and it is from here that access to the Heart becomes available in a manner that is totally unapproachable from the "noise of the third-dimension." It is from here that we are able to access the Sacred Heart, the Higher Heart, the Sanctuary of the Pink Diamond, as it is known in the Higher levels of consciousness.

The Sanctuary of the Pink Diamond

As you enter the Sacred Heart, The Sanctuary of the Pink Diamond, you do so in deep reverence. To enter the Sacred Heart a sacred Seal is opened. This Seal can only be opened by being the Love that you are. Being the Love that you are facilitates entry into the Chamber of the Hall of Crystals, where much is stored, lying dormant, waiting to be reactivated. From here, you are finally able to enter the Sacred Heart, at the center of which lies a brilliant, radiant, Pink Crystallized Light.

Within the Sanctuary of the Pink Diamond there are a number of activations that will occur; the first and most important of which is to invite the Soul back into the Heart to once again become One with the Soul.

CHAPTER 8

The Fifth-Dimension -Your Spiritual Abilities are Revealed

When you enter the fifth-dimensional consciousness you experience a full reintegration with your Higher Self and merge with your Soul. This reconnection with your higher aspects allows you to once again know yourself at a Soul level. You begin to think from Heart and act from the wisdom of your Soul. Your innate, intuitive, spiritual abilities now become fully available to you again. These include clairvoyance, telepathy, abstract intuition, and many more. You become fully conscious, accessing the wisdom and information available within the higher multidimensional aspect of that which you have always been. There is no separation.

The higher dimensions operate within fields of awareness that are not accessible to the rational third or fourth-dimensional mind. The rules, structures and means of creating in these fields of awareness are known as Alchemy, which is a natural way of life in the higher dimensions. Alchemy is defined by the Archangels as, "The ability to change the frequencies of thought, alter the harmonics of matter, and apply the elements of Love to create a desired result."

The mastering of Alchemy is found in curiosity, inquisitiveness and application: learning to utilize sound, color, and geometry to weave shape and form. Magnetism, electromagnetism, patterns of Light, feelings of beauty and higher aspects of Love all come together to form the complexities of universities as well as the simplicity of a drop of water on a morning Lily. Alchemy is the very fabric of the fifth-dimension.

There is much that changes in the fifth-dimension; consciousness becomes broader, more dynamic than anything you can imagine in the third-dimension. Physical density ends, form becomes very fluid and the structure of the physical body turns into Light. Much of your DNA is reactivated and the portion of your brain that has been dormant for so long comes alive again.

The fifth-dimension vibrates at a very high, brilliant and fast frequency range of Light, Love and great beauty. Heavy, dense thoughts and emotional vibrations such as reaction, anger, judgment, and fear cannot be held in the fifth-dimensional realm. In the fifth-dimensional frequency ranges of Light there are no limitations; all possibilities are available for creation.

Time in the fifth-dimension

Time exists once again in the fifth dimension, but in a very different configuration than previously experienced. Once fourth-dimensional Present Time is understood, time shifts into Simultaneous Time. In Simultaneous Time, all things exist in the same place at the same moment. In the fifth-dimension there are no past or future lives, no parallel or alternate lives; all that

you have ever been and ever will be are accessible in
this dimension of consciousness at the same moment.

Infinity of choices

As a citizen of the fifth-dimension you will remember
how to master every thought, every word, every action,
and every instant. As a fully conscious being of Light,
you will have multiple opportunities to expand and
continue your journey as the unique, immortal spark of
the Creator that you are. There are an infinite number of
choices, as well as infinite possibilities to choose from
in order to experience your journey.

For example, one choice is to continue experiencing
yourself as a unique, singular aspect of the Creator,
fully conscious of you. You could choose to experience
this as an Ascended Master in a different galaxy or
universe. Or have you ever considered the possibility of
becoming the consciousness of a planet or a star? You
could also choose to continue on into the seventh,
eighth and ninth-dimensions, becoming one with a
collective group consciousness, knowing all that is held
within that unique collective consciousness, and
experiencing this Oneness.

A third opportunity is to once again return to the
Oneness of All That Is; returning to the Heart of the
Creator, and experiencing yourself as the Creator
experiences Itself. These are all choices that are
available to you, and no one choice is better than any of

the others; they simply all exist within the infinite fields of endless possibilities and awareness.

CHAPTER 9

How to Enjoy the Journey

If you are reading this book you have been extraordinarily successful on your journey. It is now time to return Home.

The purpose of the Shift is to facilitate, assist and bring to you all the possibilities that will allow you to release who you are not, as well as enable you to embrace who you have always been but have forgotten. The first and most important choice is to become aware of the fact that you have choice.

This means, choosing to become conscious of being conscious; choosing to be the higher dimensional being that you are; becoming conscious and choosing to observe without being influenced by or reacting to the motion and noise around you; allowing others to act out without making their behavior personal; looking for a higher road to choose in each situation - these are the choices of the fourth-dimension. Whereas continuing to argue with or push against, choosing blame and guilt, allowing yourself to be the effect of the thoughts and emotions of others, resenting the situation you find yourself in and complaining about it over and over - these are all third-dimensional reality choices. Which do you choose?

Walking a Higher Path

When you choose to walk this higher path, you will begin to notice (if you allow yourself to) that you are beginning to think more often with your Heart and are acting from the wisdom of your Higher Mind to create a better set of choices.

When you choose to decide to follow your Heart, you discover that there are many tools, skills, and abilities that can be accessed and learned that will assist this acceleration of awakening consciousness. As you align with the Alchemy of your Heart, directed from a higher dimensional aspect of yourself, you can re-create a platform of stability and grace. From these higher vibrations of awareness much information now becomes available to you.

As you choose to master Alchemy, you begin to integrate the words of higher concepts, learning to fully comprehend words such as Happiness, Certainty, Seniority, Presence, Capable, Gracious and Command. These are not merely words to be spoken; rather, they are words to be experienced. These are Living Energy Fields of consciousness that are to be integrated and demonstrated.

The Rays of Creation

From this platform you begin to access the Rays of Creation, which form the energetic building blocks used by all aspects of the Creator to create the "All that

Is." The twelve Rays of Creation are the frequencies, sound currents, color and geometries that form and organize every adamantine particle, the basic building blocks of Universal LOVE. By learning and applying the Rays of Creation, you will learn to clear away disharmonic unconscious patterns, which magnetically bind us to the third-dimension and much more.

Simultaneous Time

As you learn to place your attention into the fourth, fifth, and sixth-dimensional thought realms, you begin to access the knowledge held within the frequencies of these higher realms of consciousness. You begin to experience Simultaneous Time, which enables you to access all the experiences of your past lives and all the wisdom of your future lives.

With this expanded knowledge and wisdom you can now change the geometry of the Octahedron into the vehicle of Light known as the Star Tetrahedron. This geometry allows for a greater range of information and the opportunity to participate in higher dimensions.

And this is just the beginning.

CHAPTER 10

The Mastering of Alchemy

This expanded knowledge opens communication with and guidance from many levels of consciousness, including the angelic, animal and elemental realms. Your imagination will open and you will experience and see things that you have never thought possible and perceive opportunities that have never been imagined.

You will have access to the many amazing and beautiful gardens and temples within the higher dimensions. In these gardens the trees sing, creating a symphony of beauty and well-being, and as their melodies fill the air with vibrational energy, not only do the colors of the leaves change each moment; they release new fragrances that have never been experienced in third-dimensional reality. As you step through the slivers of Simultaneous Time, access to the Temples of Healing and Resurrection are immediately available and you are welcomed into Temples of Wisdom, Purification and the Violet Consuming Flame.

You also begin to create new pathways within the sleep state, through the lower astral realms into the higher etheric realms, so that upon your return to the waking state, you now begin to remember where you journeyed and with whom you played as your body slept.

These are but a few of the opportunities that await you in the field of possibilities within the fifth-dimension.

CHAPTER 11

Unveiling the Experiment

This is a Grand Adventure, an adventure that was never thought to be possible. What and how we are creating is being observed from every corner of all the universes. There is amazement, admiration and great joy in the Hearts of the observers, as they watch the Grand Finale unfold. We are not only unraveling ourselves from the third-dimension; we are creating a new Home – a new "Heaven on Earth" in the higher dimensions.

And as spectacular as this is, there is more...

There is now an opportunity that was never previously imagined to be possible for these times. In co-creation with the Archangels and the Great Beings of Light there is an opportunity to bring forth a new pathway; one that is created through the Hearts of the most passionate of humanity; those who can hold the dream of bringing Heaven to Earth. This pathway is an experiment.

As the third-dimension is being dissolved, All of humanity will move forward on a path to returning "Home," leaving the third-dimension behind to become a mere reflection of a shadow gone by. The great portion of mass of consciousness that is in tangled in their fear and belief of lack will follow a path with numerous pauses in order to heal, remember and grow. As their new way of life is remembered and the Alchemy of the higher dimensions understood, they will find themselves also in the beauty of the higher dimensions. However, those who are reading this book have an opportunity to make a different choice.

The Archangels believe there is an opportunity now to provide a set of tools and a series of choices and experiences to those who ask. If chosen, an extraordinary opportunity is now possible. A pathway for this experiment has been created, and if followed, it will enable humanity to bypass the incremental steps that mass consciousness will experience. If followed, this pathway will greatly accelerate the journey of each who chooses to step upon it, and will accelerate the journey for all of humanity.

CHAPTER 12

Revealing the True Nature of the "Experiment"

The purpose of this small book is to introduce you to this new pathway, and to reveal to you the true nature of the experiment...

YOU are the experiment.

YOU are being asked to awaken and walk this accelerated pathway with the hope that as you once again become the fully conscious Being of bright Light that you are, others will see your Light and follow you back to the Heart of the Creator.

It was hoped in the year 2000 that a small group of humans could align a vibration of Light so brilliant that a crystallized doorway could be created. And because of what was done in 2012, that glimmer has become a brilliant flame of Light, which is now being firmly held by those who believe; those of you who are remembering and beginning to understand that not only are you not little, as you erroneously thought, but you are BIGGER, MORE IMPORTANT and MORE SIGNIFICANT than you have ever imagined.

And – most importantly, YOU count. YOU are the Light that appears at the top of the candle-stick for all in the house to see. And as you awaken and remember, realign, rewire and recreate yourself, your vibration is beginning to awaken the rest of the world.

Today the experiment is unfolding...and you are awakening.

Be pleased with yourself ... It is time for all to return Home

EPILOGUE

People often ask how I know what I know and how I receive the information, tools and techniques that I teach. The answer may surprise you.

Ever since I was a child I have enjoyed full recall of what happens as I asleep. Each night when I go to sleep I pass through the astral realm and experience, very consciously, the higher etheric realms, which is a most wonderful place. In these realms I get to consciously play with the Angels, the Archangels and the Great Spiritual Beings of Light. Right now, the excitement about this Shift of Consciousness that is currently taking place on Earth is the focal point of almost everyone in the higher realms.

Most mornings I awaken with full and complete memory of what occurred during the night, including where I went and whom I played with. I feel extremely blessed to be able to sit at the table with these great beings of Light and to experience this amazing orchestration of events. More importantly, however, I would also like you to know that every night YOU too sit at the same table; not as a visitor, but as an equal; for this is where you also go during those eight hours of sleep that you do not remember.

Let me also make it just as clear that whether you are just discovering this new adventure, or you have been playing the game of "bringing Heaven to Earth" for some period of time, contrary to what you have been taught to believe, YOU are very significant. You have always been very significant, and it is now time to remember who you truly are.

It is time to realign yourself, to rewire yourself, and to recreate yourself, so that you too can once again remember and re-experience all that you have forgotten you know.

It is time to remember your purpose, and to assist all the others behind you - those who are just waking up as well as those who have yet to awaken - to remember their purpose.

It has been specifically requested by the Archangels and Great Beings of Light that these tools to remembering who you are should be presented and made available to all who wish to participate in this experiment.

Since I have been asked to assist in this process, it is my desire, my passion and my privilege to provide as much information as possible. Hence you will find, on our website, many lectures, articles, tools and skills, along with audio archives and video clips offered freely for your growth, understanding and well-being.

AUTHOR JIM SELF

 **Jim Self** is often introduced as a teacher's teacher and a healer's healer. He has been leading seminars and teaching clairvoyance and personal energy management courses internationally. Jim has been featured on television, radio and in international publications.

Since childhood, Jim has retained a conscious awareness and ability to recall his experiences within the sleep state. Over the last ten years, this awareness has expanded into relationships with the Archangels, Ascended Masters and Teachers of Light. The tools and information presented in the Mastering Alchemy Program is a co-creation with these teachers and masters.

Jim walks with a foot in both worlds. At the age of twenty-six, he was elected to his first of two terms to the San Jose, CA City Council and later became the Vice Mayor. Before completing his second term, he was

asked by the president to be an advisor and the Director of US Governmental Operations for the Dept. of Energy. As an entrepreneur, he has successfully built and sold two corporations, and is the founder and current board chairman of a third.

Explore more at www.MasteringAlchemy.com

May you experience
laughter,
happiness
and much success
on your journey Home.

Printed in Great Britain
by Amazon

51812629R00033